Original title:
A House Full of Life

Copyright © 2025 Creative Arts Management OÜ
All rights reserved.

Author: Colin Leclair
ISBN HARDBACK: 978-1-80587-138-5
ISBN PAPERBACK: 978-1-80587-608-3

The Magic of Simple Gatherings

In the kitchen, spills and thrills,
Laughter echoes over silly meals.
A cat jumps high, then lands ungracefully,
The joy binds us like glue, oh so playfully.

Mismatched socks dance across the floor,
As kids flip pancakes; they want more!
Grandpa tells a tale, half true, half lost,
It's the laughter we share that counts the most.

Fables Told by the Fireside

Crackling flames and marshmallows, too,
Mom's bad jokes always come out of the blue.
A ghost story told with a wink of the eye,
As shadows on walls make the children all cry.

Sister sneezes; her s'more takes flight,
Landing more strategic than a bird in mid-flight.
Dad roars large with laughter so hearty,
While the dog snags the treat and starts a new party.

Moments of Stillness in Busyness

Amidst the chaos, a bubble bath waits,
Rubber ducks float, while time hesitates.
The doorbell rings, oh no, what a sight!
It's a neighbor with cookies, all baked just right.

Children bounce in like a whirlwind pack,
The quiet returns, just a moment to track.
A pause filled with giggles, just breathing it in,
Life's vibrant rhythm is where we begin.

The Rhythm of Familiar Days

Morning shouts merge with cereal crunch,
Socks go missing; what a funny bunch!
The dog steals a shoe, just for fun,
As we race to catch him, the laughter's begun.

Evening brings stories, all bright and loud,
Tales of our day, shared once more with the crowd.
The family's ensemble, a mishmash of sound,
It's in our little quirks where happiness is found.

Memories Etched in Time

In the kitchen, crumbs galore,
Mom's pancake flip is never a bore.
The dog dodges, a furry blur,
While the cat judges, demure and pure.

Down the hall, a classic game,
Hide and seek, it's never the same.
Dad's the best at finding us fast,
But his own hiding was never a blast!

Every corner hums a tune,
From the living room's wild balloon.
With laughter echoes filling the air,
It's the magic we all love to share.

Rooms That Breathe Shared Dreams

The bathroom's a jungle of rubber ducks,
Where shampoo bottles dance, and luck plucks.
Mirror fights with silly grins,
'Til toothpaste wars commence with wins.

In the den, games stacked high,
Cards against parents make everyone cry.
A board game battle: who's the king?
No one knows who'll win, or anything!

In the backyard, smores and smoke,
Silly stories around a pretty oak.
We roast marshmallows, burn 'em just right,
Under a sky that glows through the night.

Collective Heartbeats in Each Corner

The laundry room's a mini-zoo,
Socks mating, a mystery that's true.
A sock puppet show starts without shame,
Where my missing pair has its own claim.

The dining table shouts with glee,
Spaghetti fights and sauce fights for free.
Mom's angry looks, a clever disguise,
While we giggle and roll our eyes.

As dusk falls, tales relive and twine,
A family knot that's simply divine.
Belly laughs echo as candles glow,
In every heart, a warmth does flow.

Threads of Laughter Sewn Together

In the attic, treasures dusted and old,
Costumes spark joy, as stories unfold.
Pirate hats and glittery tiaras,
Sibling monsters in scattered pajamas.

The garage, a parking lot of time,
Antique chairs that seem to chime.
With home videos as our finest show,
Mom's dance moves? Definitely a no!

Living room cushions launched like space ships,
Trip over laughter and taste silly drips.
A symphony of giggles fills the night air,
As we share secrets, whispers laid bare.

Echoes in the Hallway

In the hall, a cat takes flight,
Chasing shadows left and right.
Mom yells, "Don't you dare to play!"
But the cat just winks and strays.

Grandpa snores in his favorite chair,
While the kids giggle without a care.
"Shh! The dragon sleeps!" they shout,
As they sneak out to roam about.

Whispering Walls

The walls do chatter, it's quite absurd,
Telling secrets without a word.
"Watch out for the mess under the bed!"
Squeals of laughter, who would have said?

They play hide-and-seek in every nook,
Finding treasures in every book.
Then there's Aunt Sally's famous stew,
A recipe that defies the crew.

The Symphony of Everyday

Morning's a dancer, full of cheer,
With breakfast tunes ringing in our ear.
Toaster pops, and toast flies high,
While coffee spills, oh my oh my!

Afternoon brings a thunderous thump,
Kids bouncing like a rubber dump.
"Did you hear that?" Dad peers around,
As the dog looks guilty, just a mound.

Laughter Between the Rooms

In one room, giggles turn to snorts,
As mischief brews in all sorts.
The bathroom door swings open wide,
With bubble battles, they cannot hide.

The dining room's a comic stage,
Full of antics that never age.
Dinner's served with cheer and clatter,
As heaven knows, it's all that matters.

Foundations of Joy

In the kitchen, pots all clank,
The dog steals toast; we give a prank.
Laughter bubbles, spills like tea,
Mom's on a wild dance spree.

Sock puppets fast on the floor,
Dad's telling tales of days of yore.
Caught in giggles, the kids all squeal,
Living here is quite the deal.

Chasing Dust Motions

The vacuum roars like it's alive,
Chasing crumbs, it loves to strive.
We run and hide behind the couch,
Dust bunnies giggle, 'Oh, what a slouch!'

Every corner holds a tale,
Cats emerge, their tails a sail.
"Not me!" they say as they prepare,
To leap and bounce without a care.

The Warmth of Togetherness

Dinner time, nine forks do clash,
Dropping peas with a loud crash.
Sister sneezes, juice goes flying,
"Oops!" she says, while the rest are crying.

Family games, a raucous night,
Board games turn into a fight.
Who knew that love could also sting,
When mom yells out, "It's not a fling!"

Rooms Filled with Echoes

Whispers dance through halls at night,
As shadows play with sheer delight.
Footsteps shuffle in a race,
Dog's chewing shoes with panache and grace.

The TV blares, a talk-show mess,
Grandpa's snoring can't impress.
Yet in these walls, a harmony,
Brings out the best, you have to see.

Ties That Bind Beyond the Door

The cat steals socks from laundry's grace,
While children race at a dizzying pace.
A dog's loud bark, a trumpet's call,
Harmony brewed in chaos for all.

Grandma's cookies hide in plain sight,
With crumbs that lead to snack time delight.
Dad's singing echoes, off-key but bright,
Voices mingle, a joyous invite.

The Dance of Everyday Chaos

Mom spins in circles, a whirlwind of chores,
While dinner simmers, love and laughter pours.
The blender roars like a lion's roar,
As kids start tangoing, searching for more.

Dishes are whirling, as if in a race,
Pasta's a slippery, delightful embrace.
Socks take flight like balloons in the air,
Caught in the chaos, not a moment to spare.

Breaths of Contentment

Coffee brews loudly, a morning decree,
While toast pops up, almost jumps with glee.
Laughter erupts, a bubbling spring,
As stories unfold, each heart takes wing.

The cat winks slyly, plotting his snack,
While tiny voices chant, "We're never going back!"
Peace in the swirl of mismatched pairs,
Finding joy in life's little affairs.

Sheltering Emotions and Elements

Rain taps lightly, a drummer's delight,
As puddles gather for jumpers' flight.
A mismatched umbrella, a bit too small,
Makes laughter echo as down they all fall.

Inside the fortress of blankets and fun,
Sibling wars waged, but friendships still won.
With fortresses built from cushions and dreams,
Every corner brims with playful schemes.

The Heart's Abode.

In the kitchen, pots do dance,
As veggies roll, they take a chance.
Cats chase crumbs with stealthy glee,
While the dog saves seats with loyalty.

The walls are painted with stories bold,
Of secret snacks, and laughter untold.
Each corner hums a silly song,
While the echo of giggles keeps us strong.

Laundry fights, with socks unmatched,
Dishes pile up, the war dispatched.
Mom just sighs, her hands on hips,
While Dad sneaks off for secret chips.

Family feuds over board games heat,
With playful jabs and playful defeat.
In this chaos, love is the prize,
And laughter sparkles like the sun in our eyes.

Echoes of Laughter in Every Room

In the den, the cat takes aim,
At paper balls, it loves the game.
Cousin Timmy boasts he's a star,
Until he trips on Dad's old car.

In the hall, we dance and spin,
The floor gives way, let the fun begin.
A bump, a fall, someone yells,
As we unleash our grandma's spells.

In the bathroom, rubber ducks unite,
While bubbles burst into silly flight.
Squeaky toys are up for grabs,
As friends become our giggling jabs.

Each room alive with playful cheer,
Shouts and whispers, loved ones near.
With every mess, a memory sticks,
In this joyful chaos, our hearts mix.

Whispers of the Hearth

The fire crackles, tales unfold,
With spooks and laughs, and food retold.
Uncle Joe spins quite the yarn,
But we all know he won't get far.

In the kitchen, cookies bake,
What's that smell? It's a sweet mistake!
Flour clouds our playful fights,
As we sneak treats under moonlight nights.

The basement hides games of old,
Where mysteries and secrets unfold.
Ghostly giggles float in the air,
As we play hide-and-seek with flair.

Gather 'round, let stories fly,
For in our hearts, the laughter's nigh.
Each chuckle woven, ties us tight,
In whispers soft, our love takes flight.

Sunlit Corners and Shadowed Nooks

Sunbeams bounce from wall to wall,
Where shadows lurk and laughter thrall.
In every nook, a treasure's found,
With silly hats and giggles all around.

The attic sings of forgotten dreams,
While laughter spills from hidden seams.
Dust bunnies play in the fading light,
As we create our own delight.

In the garden, toys lie strewn,
Amidst the flowers, a jester's tune.
The dog digs deep for praise and treats,
While siblings swap their sneaky feats.

At twilight's end, we gather near,
With funny tales and friendship dear.
In every space, our love's displayed,
In sunlit corners, fun is made.

Scent of Sunday Mornings

Pancakes flipping, syrup drips,
Socks mismatched, playful quips.
Coffee brews in wild revolt,
Cats plotting, it's their fault.

Newspaper scattered, crumbs galore,
Who spilled jam on the floor?
Laughing loud, the dog runs by,
With spaghetti strung from the sky.

Grandma's glasses, now on Dad,
He's reading comics, how very rad!
Tickles whispered, joyful screams,
Life is sweeter than it seems.

Mayhem's dance, tunes of delight,
Living rooms aglow with light.
Sundays spent, we wouldn't trade,
In this chaos, laughter's made.

The Harmony of Everyday Routines

Morning stretches, socks on heads,
Toothpaste battles, smiles instead.
Chasing kids, a wild spree,
Breakfast fun, who drank all the tea?

Door slams shut, shoes in a pile,
Chores postponed, we laugh awhile.
Grocery trips that turn to games,
Counting veggies, making names.

Dish duty, a splash and a shout,
Who can dry without a doubt?
Sweeping dust and telling tales,
Life's rhythm sets our sails.

In the whirl of the laundry spin,
Laughter bubbles, we take a win.
Every moment rings with cheer,
In our rhythm, love draws near.

Sips of Tea and Chapters Shared

Tea brews hot, stories begin,
Grandpa chuckles, where to begin?
Books piled high, a cozy nook,
Who knew life's a funny book?

Crumpets crumbling, crumbs in hair,
Someone's giggling, do we care?
Characters jump, plot twists amaze,
In our world, we're lifelong bays.

Tea leaves dance, the kettle sings,
Imaginations sprout new things.
Chapters shared, laughter loud,
In our hearts, we stand so proud.

Bookmarks fade as laughter climbs,
Life entwined with silly rhymes.
Each sip holds a tale endorsed,
In our chaos, we're well-resourced.

Memories Made in Colorful Chaos

Crayons scattered, colors bold,
Art on walls, stories told.
Sticky fingers, faces smeared,
In this mess, joy is adhered.

Dinners splashed with overcooked,
Who knew greens would be so hooked?
Laughter echoes, here and there,
Puzzle pieces everywhere.

Balloons pop in gleeful cheer,
Silly hats worn without fear.
Games of tag, laughter erupts,
In our whirlwind, time corrupts.

Memories stitched with threads of fun,
In this chaos, we are one.
Life's little moments knit so tight,
In our hearts, they shine so bright.

A Garden of Hearts

In the corner, pots all stacked,
A cactus smiles, slightly cracked.
The flowers dance in wild delight,
While gnomes argue who stays up at night.

Bees are buzzing, a loud commotion,
Chasing squirrels as they cause a notion.
Petunias gossip, tulips break bread,
As sunflowers plot to cover their heads.

Children race with muddy shoes,
Chasing butterflies, spreading bright hues.
Laughter echoes, it never ends,
In this garden, chaos transcends.

Scent of Spices and Stories

In the kitchen, scents abound,
A cinnamon tale, oh so profound.
Garlic dances with onion rings,
While herbs debate the joy that sing.

Pasta bubbling, a merry tune,
Tomatoes jive, they're not immune.
The chef's hat flies, a playful jest,
As flour fights back with zestful zest.

Guests arrive with tales to share,
Spilling laughter, a fragrant air.
Chili sneezes, it's got a flair,
Cooking up stories, spreading cheer.

Mending Broken Things

Tape and scissors, a crafty crew,
Fixing toys with colors anew.
Buttons rolling, a daring race,
While glue gets stuck, finding its place.

Socks in pairs, a missing mate,
Patches laughing at their fate.
Old shoes dancing on the shelf,
Whispering secrets to themselves.

Kids with crayons, a masterpiece,
Creating worlds where laughter's released.
Every dent tells a silly tale,
In this workshop, love won't fail.

Embracing Each Moment

Ticking clocks and playful grins,
Chasing shadows, the day begins.
Ice cream drips, a sticky cheer,
As laughter echoes far and near.

Hats get tossed in a silly toss,
While puppies plot to be the boss.
Jumping puddles, who left that there?
Smiles and giggles fill the air.

Each hug shared, a story told,
Moments cherished, never old.
In this chaos, joy looks bright,
As hearts embrace the sheer delight.

Generations Under One Roof

With grandpa's snoring like a bear's growl,
And kids racing like squirrels on a prowl.
The kitchen's a lab with snacks everywhere,
While mom's chasing crumbs and pulling her hair.

Dad's war stories mixed with tales of old,
Of how he once traded a cat for gold.
The laughter erupts like popcorn in pots,
As we dodge flying socks and mysterious spots.

The Symphony of Shared Moments

In the living room, it's a circus parade,
With a dog in a tutu and kids unafraid.
A symphony of giggles, clinks, and clatters,
As everyone joins in on the chaotic banters.

The kitchen's a war zone, flour in the air,
Mom's yelling 'Dinner!' while dad styles his hair.
We juggle the chaos, it's a comedic dance,
As we trip over toys in our merry romance.

Walls That Hold Our Stories

These walls have seen mischief, laughter, and tears,
Like when cousin Johnny hid in the gears.
The crayon doodles hold tales of great fun,
Yet sometimes we question who's winning, who's won.

Grandma's old rocking chair creaks with a grin,
While secrets are shared that spark out loud din.
Each painting and photo, a memory bright,
Of bedtime stories that stretch into night.

Roots Entwined in Cozy Spaces

In corners of chaos, love finds its nook,
With puzzles and pieces that no one can cook.
The dog's on the couch, judging our style,
While we swap funny stories, keeping it versatile.

Neighbors peek in, wondering what's the buzz,
As we all come together, just because.
A warm pot of soup and some laughter to toss,
In this patchwork of joy, we are never at a loss.

Sunbeams on the Kitchen Table

Morning light spills on crumbs,
A dance of shadows and muffins.
The cat thinks it's a hunting ground,
Chasing dust motes like old rumors.

Spoons clatter, laughter erupts,
A sibling swipes the last toast.
Coffee spills like endless tales,
While the toaster pops like popcorn.

Jams fight for prime position,
Sticky spoons and sneaky hands.
The cereal box takes a tumble,
And chaos reigns with happy chants.

Sunlight winks on every dish,
Reminding us of our wild mess.
With every snack and spilled heart,
Joy lies in the simplest parts.

Footsteps in Forgotten Corners

Dust bunnies plot in the hall,
As I step on squished fruit snacks.
Lost socks tell tales of adventures,
While the rug begs for a good shake.

Voices echo from the attic,
Old toys unite for a loud cheer.
A recliner's squeak like a witness,
Of secrets shared and dreams chased here.

The closet laughs on its own,
Hiding treasures from long ago.
Each step stirs up silly stories,
Like how that shirt was once a cape.

Footprints laid in muddy paths,
A trail of crumbs that leads to fun.
In corners where shadows linger,
Life dances, never quite done.

A Tapestry of Memories

Threads of laughter weave the air,
With stories stitched into the seams.
Grandma's quilt covers past years,
Each square holds secrets and dreams.

There's a patch from summer's picnic,
Spilled lemonade, a sticky scene.
A button from Dad's loud holidays,
A reminder of joys ever gleaned.

Stains from cooking adventures,
That time flour turned into a cloud.
Each thread is a laugh that we share,
Binding us in memories loud.

Faded colors, still so bright,
This tapestry, a joyful song.
In every stitch, life sings sweet tunes,
A fabric where we all belong.

The Heartbeat of Home

A toaster sings with morning cheer,
Eggs dance with a little jazz.
The fridge hums a lullaby tune,
While breakfast is turned into a spazz.

The couch creaks with tired laughter,
As it takes a well-deserved nap.
Remote wars start with giggles,
Pillow forts rise in a snap.

Footfalls race towards the door,
Chasing moments ready to burst.
Even the dog joins in the fray,
Barking at joy as he thirsts.

In every corner, love resides,
With echoes of silly playtime.
The heartbeat of this dear haven,
Is a rhythm forever in rhyme.

The Dance of Vibrant Disarray

Chaos reigns, socks everywhere,
Cats in hats, dancing with flair.
The dog steals lunch, what a sight,
The toddler's giggles, pure delight.

Cookies crumble, the floor's a mess,
Mom says, "Clean up!" with some stress.
But laughter echoes, hearts collide,
In this whirlwind, joy won't hide.

A plop, a spill, a funny face,
Everyone tripping in this race.
We swirl like leaves in an autumn breeze,
Caught in the fun, a joyful tease.

At day's end, the world feels right,
In cheerful chaos, hearts ignite.
With hugs and smiles, they find their way,
In this vibrant dance of the day.

Snacktime Stories and Bedside Whispers

Peanut butter smeared on the wall,
Sticky fingers chase the dog, oh what a ball!
Laughter spills with every bite,
Snacktime's never a boring sight.

Crispy crumbs in the cozy bed,
Pillows lined with dreams instead.
A tale of dragons, a pirate's quest,
Whispers of wild adventures, the best.

Juice boxes tip like tiny boats,
While bedtime stories spark wild thoughts.
"Just one more snack!" the kids all plead,
"Monsters under the bed?" They both concede.

The clock ticks loud, it's getting late,
With giggles and wiggles, they just can't wait.
Through snack and stories, bonds grow tight,
Bedtime fun turns into pure delight.

A Gaze Through the Garden Gate

We peek through the gate, oh what a scene,
Bouncing bunnies where grass grows green.
Chasing the shadows, butterflies swoop,
The garden's alive with a playful troop.

Tomatoes tumble, the weeds have a dance,
The sunflowers reach to sway and prance.
A frog leaps high, the birds join in,
A chorus of chuckles, it's time to begin.

With watering cans and muddy shoes,
Each little sprout has its own humorous news.
The veggies giggle, the flowers play tricks,
Pulling weeds feels like a garden mix.

From petals to puddles, joy runs free,
A stroll down the path brings laughter and glee.
We wave to the squirrels, the blooms all agree,
In our garden's embrace, there's room for spree.

Echoes of Generations Past

Grandma's stories spin like a top,
She spins her yarns while the soup does plop.
With every chuckle, the kitchen glows,
Mixing laughter with the smells that flow.

Dad plays a tune on the old guitar,
While the kids march in with their make-believe war.
The past comes alive with each silly sound,
In this family chaos, love's tightly wound.

Old photos slip from the album pile,
Each snapshot whispers a funny style.
"Remember when?" leads to big grins,
As memories bubble, the joy begins.

The clock ticks loud, but time stands still,
With echoes of laughter, great tales to fill.
Generations dance, in moments vast,
We find our roots in the fun of the past.

The Palette of Family Life

In the kitchen, laughter brews,
Colors splatter, joys and blues.
Socks on the ceiling, toys in the stew,
Who needs a canvas? We've got a zoo!

Pasta fights on Tuesday nights,
Spaghetti flung like airborne kites.
Mom's spaghetti sauce just might ignite,
An art exhibit of marital sights!

The fridge is a portal, it opens wide,
With leftovers that dare to collide.
Not quite gourmet, we take them in stride,
Our hearts are the recipes, baked with pride.

Grandpa's puns, they age like fine wine,
Catchphrase battles, always on time.
Who knew suburbia could be so divine?
In this house, chaos is simply sublime!

Joys and Sorrows Under One Sky

Under one roof, we dance and cry,
Juggling dreams, giving it a try.
Laundry mountains piled so high,
Who knew socks had wings to fly?

Dinner times, we're quite the scene,
Veggies fly like a circus dream.
Kids make art, in ketchup they beam,
Life's a comedy, or so it seems!

Fights over toys like grand debates,
The cat's the judge, with royal traits.
Her royal decree, 'No more debates!'
Until snack time, when all's up for mates!

In the backyard, we build a fort,
With pillows, blankets, a grand resort.
Imaginations blend, a true cohort,
In our silly world, we're never short!

Nests Built on Dreams

Nestled close, a quirky team,
Pillow fights and ice cream dreams.
Building castles, oh what a scheme,
Jumping on beds, a child's theme!

Cereal spills, a crunchy delight,
The cat dodges, takes flight at night.
Living to laugh, we take our plight,
In a world of giggles, all feels right.

Plans for tomorrow, dressed in absurd,
Unicorns talk, or so it's heard.
While chores await, we'll not be deterred,
A bubble bath party, dreams interspurred!

With crayons and markers, art's our spark,
Our walls are scribbled, a colorful arc.
This nest is our haven, never too stark,
In this realm, we're here to embark!

Conversations in the Quiet Hours

In the twilight, whispers sway,
We huddle close, our worries stray.
The dog snores loudly—a symphony play,
While popcorn kernels decide to ballet.

Sippy cups under the couch reside,
Each secret spilled, like a wild tide.
Cousins share tales, eyes open wide,
Imagination flies, no need to hide.

The moon peeks in through a close-lipped vow,
Pajama-clad stories, sacred now.
With flashlights in hand, we take a bow,
In the theater of dreams, we all avow.

Despite the chaos, peace is near,
Understanding blooms with every cheer.
Quiet hours, precious and dear,
In this family, love is clear.

A Canvas of Lives Intertwined

In the fridge, a mystery brew,
Leftovers danced, what a curious view.
Socks in pairs, but one goes astray,
Laundry monsters playing all day.

The cat claims the couch, a soft throne,
While kids toss pillows, laughter is grown.
Spilled juice becomes a rainbow blend,
Every moment, a twist and a bend.

Flickers of Joy

Cookies baked with a pinch of chaos,
Flour clouds drift, oh what a loss!
The dog chases the tail of a child,
Giggles abound, this vibe is wild.

Dancing with brooms, cleaning spree,
Funny faces made in glee.
Echoes of life, each moment a cheer,
While grandpa snores, oblivious near.

Unspoken Secrets Beneath the Roof

Whispers passed at the dinner table,
Who ate the cake? Now, that's a fable.
The rubber chicken sits by the phone,
A comical king on a peculiar throne.

Under the stairs, the ghosts hold court,
Sharing their tales of a lively sport.
A jar of pickles, the family debates,
Are they a snack or just for laughs' fates?

Radiance in the Quiet

A glow worm disco lights up the night,
As a snoring dad becomes a delight.
Midnight snacks, a treasure hunt,
Found half a sandwich, that's quite the stunt.

Ticklish toes under blankets so warm,
A tick-tock race, silly creatures swarm.
In the soft moments, laughter ignites,
Life's little quirks make the best sights.

The Pulse of Everyday Gatherings

In the kitchen, crumbs galore,
Laughter spills from every door.
The dog steals a sock in the fray,
Who knew chaos could be this way?

Silly games that make us grin,
Each round a search for where to pin.
Grandma's stories, lovingly tall,
We practice our skills - how to fall!

Tales of mishaps, a loud reprise,
As uncle tries to juggle pies.
Soda fountains, splashing bright,
Even the cat joins in the fight.

With every spill, we're taken high,
Who thought chaos would make us fly?
From kitchen to yard, we all convene,
In this circus, we're truly seen.

Memories Woven in Wall Paint

The walls whisper of moments past,
With crayon doodles, wild and fast.
Fingerprints of little hands sprawl,
On every corner, memories call.

The paint peels like our goofy pranks,
Colorful marks from countless thanks.
A masterpiece of stains and cheer,
The history of laughter hangs here.

Each scuff tells tales of dance and play,
A foot-stomp here, a water fight there.
Echoes of giggles fill the air,
This patchwork of life, we proudly share.

The portraits sway in sunlight's beam,
A funny face is just the theme.
In our humble art gallery show,
Every stroke, a legacy we sow.

The Charm of Multicolored Lives

In this blend of hearts and souls,
Every quirk plays unique roles.
From mismatched socks to silly hats,
A blend so rich, like spats of spats.

Our pet turtle has his own throne,
With eyes that twinkle like they've grown.
He's the king of all our mess,
In his court, there's never stress.

Jokes bounce around like bouncing beans,
Tickling ribs and splitting seams.
Grandma's dance moves, oh so fly,
Making even the cat say, 'Why?'

In colors bright, our stories weave,
Threads of laughter, do not leave.
With each twist and twirl we say,
Life's a party, come what may!

Footsteps on Worn Floors

The floors creak in a merry tune,
With every step, our lives commune.
Sneakers squeak, the carpet fidgets,
This is life, with all its widgets.

Pacing by with sticky snacks,
A trail of crumbs, a path of stacks.
Little feet in a mad parade,
Worn-out shoes with memories made.

Echoes dance where stories play,
Laughter lingers, come what may.
We trip and tumble, it's quite the show,
Each clumsy fall helps our hearts grow.

In the rhythm of those footprints bare,
The joy of living is always there.
With each shuffle, laugh, and sigh,
We are the reason these floors comply.

Room for Each Heart

In the kitchen, spills and mess,
The cat thinks it's a place to dress.
With flour on noses, joy does rise,
As we all cook with silly ties.

A living room dance, we start to sway,
Tripping on toes in a silly way.
With laughter echoing through the night,
Each tumble brings more delight!

Upstairs, the kids attempt to hide,
But stealing cookies fills them with pride.
Under the beds and in the nooks,
Life's treasures lie like storybooks.

In corners, toys have thrown a party,
A dinosaur dance, oh, that's so hearty!
Each room's a stage, a new surprise,
Where fun and chaos always flies!

The Canvas of Our Togetherness

Spilled paint on a canvas blank,
Laughing as we try to prank.
With splatters bright and colors bold,
Our masterpiece, a sight to behold.

The living room, it comes alive,
With puppet shows that make us dive.
The couch, a ship, on seas so wide,
Our pirate crew with laughter and pride.

In the garden, we plant our dreams,
Sunflowers peak, or so it seems.
With dirt on hands and smiles so sly,
Our garden grows, oh me, oh my!

From kitchen bakes to night-time tales,
Every hour, our laughter sails.
In this home, joy always stays,
Colors bright in all our ways!

Faded Photos and Fresh Laughs

Old photos stuck on the fridge's door,
Every face, a memory to explore.
With goofy grins and silly hats,
Each snapshot shows how time chats.

In the attic, treasures we find,
A box of trinkets, stories entwined.
With laughter erupting from dusty bins,
We share tales of our childhood sins.

A crazy hair day, that purple dye,
A hairstyle that made us laugh and cry.
Each tale told with goofy delight,
Faded memories, so precious, so bright.

As the stories loop and repeat,
With every laugh, our hearts skip a beat.
In this chaos, we find our art,
Faded photos that warm the heart!

Echoing Joys Through Time

In the halls where laughter lingers,
The past dances on our fingers.
We hear the echoes of playful shouts,
Through rooms filled with love, no doubts.

In the backyard, slip and slide,
With squeals of joy too hard to hide.
Water fights and games galore,
Our giggles bounce from door to door.

On rainy days, we build a fort,
With pillows stacked for our own court.
Whispers giggle in secret praise,
Imagination sparks and plays.

As memories swirl in colors bright,
Our hearts aglow in soft moonlight.
Together we laugh, in fun we climb,
Echoing joys that last through time!

Spaces Painted with Affection

In every corner, laughter hides,
The cat claims rules, while the dog decides.
A mix of chaos, joy, and glee,
Where socks are missing, that's the key.

The plants are on a gossip spree,
Telling tales of the bee's and tree's.
Each wall holds whispers, bright and bold,
Of birthday candles and stories told.

Kids run wild with ice-cream smiles,
Searching for treasure in endless piles.
The fridge hums tunes of midnight snacks,
While dad's jokes meet with witty cracks.

The Comfort of Open Doors

Open doors invite a cheeky breeze,
Neighbors pop in for a cuppa with ease.
Laughter spills like tea on the floor,
While unexpected guests ask for more.

In the yard, a trampoline lies low,
Even grandma joins in the bouncing show.
The garden blooms with silly signs,
Saying, 'Ring the bell, but knock in lines!'

Socks on the line wave like flags,
Here, even dust bunnies wear snazzy rags.
With every knock, another tale starts,
In this haven where laughter imparts.

Ties Stronger than Timber

Bouncing on beams, we play all day,
Strong ties hold us in a funny way.
Like spaghetti mixed with one big smile,
We're twisted and turned, it's all worthwhile.

Mom's secret recipe? A pinch of fun!
Where kids dream big and dog plays run.
A fort built with sheets, pillows, and glee,
Our fortress stands strong, just wait and see!

Worn-out toys tell stories of flight,
As we gather 'round the glow of night.
In this place, joy can never sever,
Our ties will last forever and ever.

Stories Told over Rushing Rivers

By the creek, we splash like wild fish,
Trading giggles for every wish.
With sticks as swords, we conquer the stream,
Each splash, a laugh, a bubbling dream.

Grandpa spins tales of heroes great,
While ducks quack in a feathery state.
The water races, full of delight,
We chase it down, oh what a sight!

With frogs as singers and stones for a crown,
We build our castle, never a frown.
In the symphony of nature's play,
We find our joy in every sway.

Windows Framed with Life's Stories

Through the glass, the sun does peek,
In here, even shadows squeak.
Old photos smile from the walls,
Where laughter dances and sometimes falls.

Cats on windowsills, they purr,
Chasing sunbeams that start to blur.
Neighbors wave with silly grins,
As the daily chaos begins.

Rain dances, yet inside we cheer,
Pajama parties bring us near.
Tales of a cat stuck in a tree,
Life unfolds, wild and free.

With each glance, more stories unfold,
In every crevice, laughter told.
Windows frame our zany crew,
Where funny moments always brew.

Bonds Woven Like a Quilt

Like patches stitched with love and care,
Each quirk and giggle fills the air.
From cooking fails to midnight chats,
We share our lives like bouncing cats.

Grandma's recipes, a little messy,
Baking bread makes us all feel dressy.
Fingers sticky with the dough,
Between our laughs, the flour goes!

Family game night, we all compete,
Until someone takes a funny seat.
With every roll of the dice, we cheer,
Love grows strong with each silly year.

Our quilt is vibrant, stitched with ease,
Bright colors made from memories.
Together woven, our lives collide,
Laughter's thread is our true guide.

The Enchantment of Familiar Voices

Mornings start with sleepy hums,
As toast pops like playful drums.
Silly banter flies through the air,
Familiar voices, beyond compare.

Dad cracks jokes, and we all groan,
But secretly, we love their tone.
Mom sings softly, a funny tune,
As the sun dances with the moon.

At dinner, we're a noisy bunch,
Mixing stories with every lunch.
Grandpa's tales of when he was young,
Leave us laughing before we're done.

Voices woven in laughs and sighs,
Echo through the evenings' skies.
Every corner filled with each sound,
In our world, joy is found.

Echoing Footsteps in the Hallway

Little feet that race and run,
Chasing giggles, what a fun!
Echoes bounce off every wall,
In the hallway, we hear it all.

The dog trots with a happy bark,
And challenges kids to a chase in the dark.
With every corner, a new surprise,
It's a cartoonish dance of lives.

Socks go flying, chaos reigns,
As the cat plots her playful gains.
With every thud and every squeak,
Our home's alive with joy we seek.

Footsteps echo, a rhythmic sound,
Filled with laughter, pure joy abound.
In our world, the heart does play,
Every step brightens the day.

The Story of Light and Shadow

In a corner, dust bunnies dance,
As if they're on a carefree prance.
The cat plots a stealthy attack,
While the sneaky dog plans his comeback.

Lamps flicker like they're in a play,
Casting shadows that drift and sway.
They whisper secrets of silly mischief,
While we munch on popcorn, feeling adrift.

Under the table, giggles arise,
As children craft grand, wild surprise.
The light chases the shadow's dark heel,
In this show, life always feels surreal.

With a beam and a wink, the nights unfold,
Every moment a story waiting to be told.
In our realm of laughter, time flies by,
A symphony of chaos, oh my, oh my!

Embracing Warmth in Chilly Evenings

The fireplace crackles with gentle glee,
As marshmallows float in cocoa tea.
Someone's sock has gone awry,
It's on the cat, oh my, oh my!

Blankets pile high, like a mountain bold,
Underneath, we gather, feeling bold.
Tickling toes as hot chocolate spills,
Laughter erupts, our hearts get thrills.

Outside the window, the snowflakes swirl,
Inside, we spin in a giddy twirl.
Chilly winds knock, they're sure to fail,
For warmth and giggles always prevail.

We sing off-key, legends of old,
Every story embellished, grandly told.
In this cozy escape, we're foolishly rich,
Wrapped in warmth, we forget every glitch!

Treasures Hidden Beneath the Stairs

Boxes stacked in a clumsy array,
Forgotten toys that once joined the fray.
An old shoe, a giggle, a pirate's hat,
Adventures await in places like that!

Trip over treasures, who put them there?
A sock puppet army, ready to dare.
Each corner whispers secrets untold,
A time machine of memories, pure gold.

Dust-covered gems, oh what a sight,
Here lurk relics from every night.
Curiosities stacked like a wild dream,
It's a cave of treasures, or so it would seem.

With every find, a chuckle erupts,
Old stories revive, new laughter erupts.
Beneath the stairs, we quest and explore,
Finding joy in the past, forevermore!

The Harmony of Clashing Interests

In the kitchen, an argument brews,
A pickle vs a cookie, who really knew?
Spices tumble, flour flies high,
With a dash of chaos, we whip up a pie.

One wants a feast, a grand buffet,
While another declares, 'Just pizza today!'
The oven hums a cheeky tune,
As decisions waltz beneath the moon.

Plates clash, but smiles abound,
In every corner, laughter resounds.
For every debate, a compromise found,
In this lively mess, joy knows no bound.

Conflict and joy in glorious swirl,
A dance of preferences, as flavors twirl.
In our kitchen orchestra, let's take a chance,
For even clashing interests can lead to a dance!

Fragile Dreams and Warm Hugs

In the morning, socks on the floor,
Cheerios spilled, what a chore.
Cats chase shadows, time to zoom,
Tiptoe, don't wake dad, he'll fume.

Lemonade stands, with too much zest,
Cousins argue who's the best.
Grandma's cookies, slightly charred,
Who knew baking could be so hard?

Puppy prancing, tail wagging wide,
Tripping over, it's a fun ride.
Time for naptime, eyes in a daze,
Dreams of dancing in a silly haze.

Sunlight fades, the day now slowed,
Stories shared on the winding road.
Laughter echoes, a sweet embrace,
In this chaos, we find our place.

The Dance of Shadows

Silly shadows play on the wall,
Dancing like they're having a ball.
The dog joins in with a goofy bark,
Granddad trips, that's quite a spark.

Tangled lights for the party tonight,
Kids run wild, what a funny sight.
Mom's lost her shoe, it's under the couch,
Dad's pretending to be a grouchy grouch.

Sing-alongs with off-key notes,
In Halloween costumes, they wear their coats.
Farts and giggles, a raucous clatter,
Who noticed the cake? Oh, splatter!

As night falls, the shadows creep,
Into our hearts, the memories seep.
A dance of joy, in whispers and sighs,
In this quirky chaos, laughter never dies.

The Chorus of Family

Breakfast chaos, forks on the floor,
Sister blares, "I just want more!"
Toast flies high, the dog makes a catch,
Smile at the mess, it's a perfect match.

Dinner time comes, we gather round,
Olive spills, laughter is found.
Mom spills wine, what a big splash,
Dad cracks a joke, we all laugh in a flash.

Hugs exchanged, and battles fought,
Who stole the pudding? A question wrought.
Pajama wars in the middle of night,
A family chorus, everything feels right.

As bedtime approaches, chaos still reigns,
With tales of dragons and silly trains.
Together we shout, though every note's rough,
In this goofy symphony, we've got enough.

Ghosts of Laughter Past

In the attic, old toys sit still,
Remembered giggles, oh what a thrill.
A ghost of childhood, peeks in to play,
Whispers of fun come back every day.

Mom's wedding dress, a comical sight,
We all giggle at the sheer delight.
Dust bunnies dancing, like they own the floor,
Granddad snores loud, we all want more.

Grandma's stories, filled with sass,
Of kitchen mishaps and falling glass.
Each laughter echo, a spirit alive,
Remembering moments, where joy can thrive.

Even in silence, we feel them near,
The ghosts of laughter, always here.
In every corner, their joy remains,
In this wild home, love never wanes.

Gathering Around the Table

In this realm of crumbs and spills,
Chairs creak with tales and thrills.
Unruly laughter, food flying high,
Someone wrestles a pasta pie.

A fork's a sword, a spoon's a shield,
In this battlefield, joy is revealed.
Gravy rivers and salad forts,
Bellyaches turn into retorts.

Grandma's pie with a secret twist,
Cousins argue, don't get missed.
Who stole the last bite of cake?
Awkward silence, for goodness' sake!

We gather, we feast, we chat and cheer,
Like a circus, it's what we hold dear.
With each bite, a story unfurls,
In the chaos, our laughter swirls.

The Heartbeat of Familiar Shelters

Where socks vanish and toys take flight,
Chaos reigns from morning to night.
The cat's on the table, a toast with cheer,
To hiccups and flops, oh how we steer!

Mom's on a mission, a kitchen galore,
Dad's on the sofa, adventures to score.
Little ones giggle with puzzling delight,
As flying snacks capture the night.

Old photos hang, with tales of yore,
Every glance, we remember more.
Siblings bicker like cats and dogs,
But love's the glue in this land of fogs.

In these walls, stories bloom bright,
Welcome to a whimsical sight.
With each quirk, our family vibes,
In this haven, our joy imbibes.

Windows to Our Togetherness

The window panes hold a view so quaint,
With grass stains and laughter, no hint of faint.
Neighbors glance and chuckle a bit,
As we juggle life, that's how we fit.

Outside the world spins, fast and wild,
Inside, we're simply a fortunate child.
Each little face tells a tale so grand,
With silly dances, we take a stand.

Sunshine spills through, a warm embrace,
In this chaos, we all find grace.
With open arms, and hearts in bloom,
We chase our worries away from the room.

So let the rain drum on our roof,
Here's where we gather, it's living proof.
Through laughs and mess, we weave our thread,
In every crack of our cozy spread.

Echoes of Shared Secrets

Whispers float like bubbles and glide,
As secrets mingle, laughter won't hide.
In corners we plot, with eyes so bright,
Stealing cookies in the still of the night.

The hallway holds a spirit of jest,
Shared giggles keeping us ever blessed.
Grandpa's tales of his youth mischief,
Each funny nuance, a joyful gift.

In closets we hide, peeking outside,
Cheeks stuffed with treats, heads filled with pride.
Knock-knock jokes danced on our lips,
While inside our hearts, the love just flips.

Let's gather 'round, let the stories flow,
In this quilt of life, we stitch and sew.
Here's to the echoes that never cease,
In this bundle of joy, we find our peace.

The Storybook of Us

In the kitchen, pots dance with glee,
A cat wearing socks, oh what a sight!
Children chase fairy tales up the tree,
While parents chase after the bedtime light.

The fridge hums tunes of yesterday's spat,
A carrot's a nose, pancakes on the floor.
Laughter erupts like confetti in a hat,
Every moment feels like searching for more.

The dog steals a sandwich, thinks it's a feast,
As shoes turn to boats in puddles galore.
Grandma recounts tales, a very good beast,
With each wild adventure, we love her more.

And as stars peek in, peeking shyly above,
We gather, recounting our comical spree.
In the book of our hearts, it fits like a glove,
Each smile, each giggle, our sweetest decree.

Lanterns of Love and Laughter

Balloons float upward, as birds catch a ride,
Tacos turn flying saucers at play.
With crayons and costumes, we let giggles slide,
As puppies chase shadows and frolic all day.

A dance-off breaks out in the living room space,
With grandpa doing the twist, what a show!
The plants seem to chuckle, a green leafy grace,
While socks play hide and seek, stealing the flow.

Our game of charades brings the house to a roar,
Each guess gets wilder, oh what a bluff!
From pirates to aliens, we're never a bore,
As laughter keeps building, there's never enough.

When night falls at last, as lanterns glow bright,
Stories fly past like fireflies in the air.
In this chaotic realm, everything feels right,
With love and laughter, we find joy everywhere.

Portraits of Connection

The dining room table, a canvas of cheer,
With spaghetti paintings and smiles galore.
Each fork's a brush, though there's sauce on the ear,
Artistic endeavors that we all explore.

Mismatched socks tell stories of playful fights,
While the clock ticks in rhythm with hiccups and bray.
The dog snores louder than thunderous nights,
In this cozy gallery, every moment's at play.

We craft crown-like hats from leftover brown bags,
And boast of our wins, but the dogs steal the show.
The grand finale ends with a chorus of tags,
As cake gets devoured, oh sweet overflow!

Each portrait tells tales of wild escapades,
Preserving the laughter we never outgrew.
In this chaotic haven where joy always wades,
Together forever, as artists, we drew.

Warmth Between the Beams

The sunbeams are tickling dust bunnies' heads,
As the couch becomes a spaceship ablaze.
In a blanket fort kingdom, we weave silly threads,
Imaginary realms fill our adventurous days.

With cookies on duty, baking clouds in the sky,
And giggles exploding like fireworks bright.
A family of monsters, we shriek and we sigh,
Finding joy in each corner, under pillows, in flight.

In the attic, a treasure of hats we explore,
Building castles while giggling, trolls guard the stairs.
The walls share our secrets, each laugh we adore,
As warmth fills the rooms, safe from worldly cares.

So here's to the chaos that brings us together,
Where each heart's a lantern, glowing and free.
Through messy adventures, like birds of a feather,
We dance in the laughter that sings between me.

A Nest of Chattering Souls

In the corner, socks go missing,
A cat prances, oh so flissing.
The kids are arguing, who's to blame,
While Uncle Joe plays a silly game.

Echoes bounce off every wall,
"Whose turn is it?" becomes a brawl.
With laughter spilling from each room,
Our noisy nest is full of zoom!

Spaghetti sauce on the ceiling,
And Auntie Pam's new dance is revealing.
Just when peace starts to take its vow,
A trumpet blares—who gave that cow?

In this chaos where joy resides,
Love and laughter are our guides.
Through shrieks and squeaks and playful yells,
Together we weave our quirky spells.

The Warmth Within Fragile Walls

Beneath the roof, the giggles soar,
As rabbit ears are worn once more.
Mom's spaghetti's turned into goo,
While Dad insists, "It tastes like a stew!"

Cousins race like lightning bolts,
While Grandpa boasts of his old faults.
The little ones, in paint they slosh,
Creating masterpieces—what a posh!

Our blankets are forts, our pillows are shields,
In this brave land, laughter yields.
The neighbors shake their heads in glee,
"What's that ruckus? Oh, let it be!"

Even fragile walls can't contain,
This joyful chorus—oh, what a strain!
With clatter, chatter, and playful brawls,
Home's warmth spreads beyond the walls.

Threads of Laughter Weaving Us Together

In every room, a joke is spun,
Where puns and giggles intertwine for fun.
A game of charades erupts in glee,
While Grandma claims victory in her spree!

Spaghetti fights break out with cheer,
As siblings battle without fear.
Each thread of laughter, a bond so tight,
Creating a fabric of pure delight.

'Who left the fridge open?' the echo calls,
Hidden snacks in the saddest of halls.
The cat just yawns, unimpressed by the show,
While we all enjoy this radiant glow.

With every quirk, we find our place,
In laughter's arms, there's warm embrace.
A house full of giggles, a haven of cheer,
Where threads of joy bring us always near.

The Embrace of Shared Silences

At times we sit in silence rare,
With popcorn flying, caught mid-air.
Eyes darting as we hear a sip,
Then laughter spills from every lip.

Our quiet moments, a funny twist,
Like when great-Grandpa starts to insist
That socks should never see the sun,
We hold our snickers, oh, what fun!

Shared silences like soft shoe shuffles,
As every little heartbeat ruffles.
In these pauses, the smiles grow wide,
In the hush of our home, we find our stride.

As bedtime stories come to rest,
We share our secrets, feeling blessed.
In stillness, we weave our bonds anew,
Together in laughter—just me and you.

Crayon Scribbles and Coffee Stains

Fading crayon myths on the wall,
A coffee stain race, who's gonna fall?
Socks in the air, a wild dance,
Mom's on the hunt, but they took a chance.

Cats on the counters, they plot and scheme,
Finding the snacks, living the dream.
Kids toss their toys, it's a grand ballet,
Then giggles erupt, come join the fray!

Pancake battles, syrupy thrill,
Who'll have the biggest, who'll take the spill?
Chasing the dog, with a pizza slice,
The chaos unfolds, oh isn't it nice?

Marking on walls, what a cute mess,
Each scribble an ode, we must confess.
Through laughter and snickers, we'll sing our tune,
In this candy-colored afternoon!

Windows to Laughter

Sunbeams break through, kids play outside,
Jumping on beds, oh what a ride!
Sneaking some cookies, with crumbs on their face,
A chorus of giggles fills up the space.

Neighbors with frowns, just shake their heads,
While we build castles using our beds.
Splashes in puddles, the dog joins in,
Who knew that chaos could feel like a win?

Dance-offs at dinner, let's not be shy,
'Round the table, we'll shimmy and fly.
Chasing our shadows, under the moon,
Boisterous whispers, a joyful tune.

Windows like portals, where dreams take flight,
Through laughter and antics, we shine so bright.
Dear friends and family, gather together,
In this quilt of moments, let's bond forever!

Conversations at Dusk

Under the twilight, secrets are spun,
Who took the last cupcake? Oh, this is fun!
Silly debates, who's the favorite cat?
Mom's rolling her eyes, but she's loving the chat.

Crickets are singing their evening song,
While the kids argue who's right and who's wrong.
"Let's build a fort!" "You're not the boss!"
Then laughter erupts, as they totally cross.

A movie of shadows on the old garden gate,
Each face illuminated, by friendly fate.
Hour by hour, our hearts take flight,
In these simple moments, everything's right.

As stars twinkle softly, we all take a pause,
In this world of chatter and playful applause.
Tomorrow's adventures, oh what will they bring?
But tonight's fully booked, with joy on a swing!

Shelves of Stories

Books stacked high, adventures galore,
Stories leap out, begging for more.
Monsters and wizards, knights in a quest,
Each page a promise, a magical jest.

Shelf of the brave, with tales yet untold,
Who knew that dust could sparkle like gold?
The dog wants to chew on a paperback tale,
While the kids set forth on a treasure trail.

Giggles erupt from the corner so small,
The cats are the heroes, who answer the call.
Lines of pure nonsense, wisdom with fun,
In this whirlwind realm, we're never quite done.

Each tale spins laughter, each chapter a grin,
Imagination runs wild; just let it begin.
The shelf holds our memories, happily stored,
In this funny domain, we're endlessly bored!

www.ingramcontent.com/pod-product-compliance
Lightning Source LLC
Chambersburg PA
CBHW051735290426
43661CB00123B/325